Mollie Miaowsings

A Pussy's Stories and Thoughts

Catherine Murray

Copyright © 2022 Catherine Murray.

All rights reserved. No part of this book may be used or reproduced by any means, graphic, electronic, or mechanical, including photocopying, recording, taping or by any information storage retrieval system without the written permission of the author except in the case of brief quotations embodied in critical articles and reviews.

Balboa Press books may be ordered through booksellers or by contacting:

Balboa Press
A Division of Hay House
1663 Liberty Drive
Bloomington, IN 47403
www.balboapress.co.uk
UK TFN: 0800 0148647 (Toll Free inside the UK)
UK Local: 02036 956325 (+44 20 3695 6325 from outside the UK)

Because of the dynamic nature of the Internet, any web addresses or links contained in this book may have changed since publication and may no longer be valid. The views expressed in this work are solely those of the author and do not necessarily reflect the views of the publisher, and the publisher hereby disclaims any responsibility for them.

Any people depicted in stock imagery provided by Getty Images are models, and such images are being used for illustrative purposes only.
Certain stock imagery © Getty Images.

ISBN: 978-1-9822-8494-7 (sc)
ISBN: 978-1-9822-8495-4 (e)

Print information available on the last page.

Balboa Press rev. date: 02/26/2022

BALBOA.PRESS
A DIVISION OF HAY HOUSE

Contents

Chapter 1 Who We Are 1

Chapter 2 Candy—the Pest—Arrives 5

Chapter 3 Terrible Teens Kitten 7

Chapter 4 Planning and Plotting 13

Chapter 5 Computer Capers 18

Chapter 6 Lockdown 21

Chapter 7 Aunties 26

Chapter 8 Visits to the Vet 29

Chapter 9 Cheerio for Now 35

Chapter 1

Who We Are

Miaow. Hello. My name is Mollie. I am big, black, and beautiful. I also have a pedigree. Yes, a real one in writing. I am a British Shorthair cat, and I know that I am a touch of class.

I live in a flat with my mum, called Catherine (Cath for short). I know her as Mum. She tells me that I am a "mummy's girl" or "Mum's girl". I share my flat with a pest called Candy

Candy has a tale (not just a tail) of his own. He was born on a farm. He is a tiger- striped cat, which I understand is a very unusual marking. I heard that all his littermates were tiger- striped as well. Mum says she is glad that she did not call him Tiger because he is a scaredy cat, very timid. He loves Mum, but the minute she stands up, he jumps onto the furniture or on top of the computer printer—anywhere high up. Mum says that because he was born on a farm, he is not "well socialised", whatever that is. She thinks that his mum told him to be wary of humans.

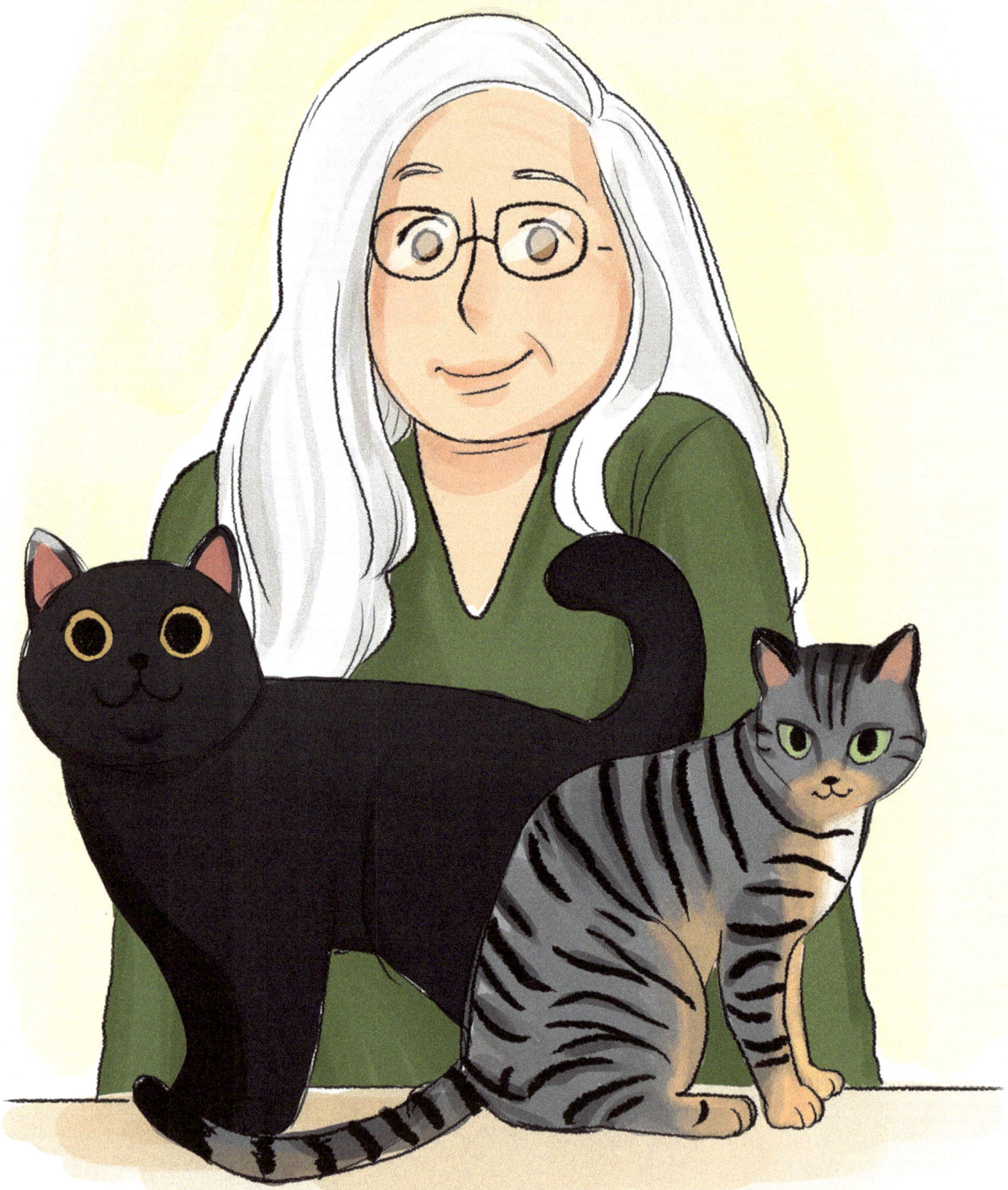

Mum also says that he is half feral because he was a farm cat. He is not wild but not really used to being with people. Once Mum is in bed, he jumps up and cuddles in. That does not always meet with my approval, but more about that later.

I am eleven years old now, and I have lived with Mum for eight of those years. My first owners did not really understand cats. They got tired of me and took me to the Cats Protection rehoming centre, saying that, and I quote, "She doesn't do anything." Well, that was not strictly true. I had trained them well, and I ate! Too much actually. When Mum adopted me at the age of three, I weighed over seven kilos, which I heard Mum say was, "the weight of some babies." Mum's first task was to put me on a strict diet. Yes, a very strict one. Mum is not a foodie herself, so it was easier for her to discipline me. Within a few months, the vet was thrilled to find that I was a slim, trim, five kilos, which is what a girl of my size is supposed to be.

Once I was slim and trim, I had more energy, and Mum learnt that I was actually a very playful girl. I am also very affectionate and simply love to be cuddled. I also love to have my ears tickled, and when I am in the mood, to have my tummy rubbed. My idea of heaven is sleeping with Mum when she goes to bed. Sometimes I have big arguments with the pest about who sleeps where. I will tell you more about that later. After I had lived with Mum for two years, she decided that I was lonely. She was out and about quite a bit of the time, and as our flat is on the third floor, and the close has locked doors, I cannot go into the garden. I keep telling Mum that I would like a garden by trying to get out of the balcony door on sunny days. Mum says she's sorry that we cannot go into the garden, but at least we have the balcony in the summer.

Anyway, Mum saw an advertisement saying that tigerstriped kittens were available for sale. This reminded Mum of her childhood cat, who was tiger- striped too. (Her name was Tibs.) Mum decided to buy a kitten to keep me company. That is when Candy (the pest), arrived. Mum was probably right about me being lonely at the time because she was out quite a lot at somewhere called university.

Chapter 2

Candy—the Pest—Arrives

I vividly remember the day that Candy arrived. Mum was busy in the morning. She had bought a new cat dish, and another cat bed. Now we had three. Yes, three in the living room, although one could double up as a footstool or a storage place for light things like newspapers. Mum's previous cat, Premie (short for Premier, who was found straying at, guess where, the Premier Inn) had liked it. I don't really use it very much at all, and I don't think Candy has even tested it out. With the arrival of a third cat bed, I had an idea that something was afoot, but I didn't really know what.

The lady arrived with a cat carrier from which she produced a tiny, tiny, tiger- striped kitten. He was so small that both Mum and the lady thought he must have some more growing to do. As it turned out, he didn't grow all that much, so I am much bigger than he is.

I have never had kittens of my own, but I had been around a bit in my eight years. I absolutely loved having him to cuddle into and to groom. I showed him where the kitty litter was and, of course, the feeding dishes in the kitchen. That was easy because he followed me like a shadow. We cuddled into each other, and I groomed him. At that time Mum thought he was a she, as that was what she had been told. Hence the name Candy.

All that changed when Mum took him to the vet for his second shot. Mum introduced Candy as a girl. The vet started his examination and then said to Mum, "I have news for you. He is a he." The vet and Mum laughed. Mum said that she didn't think she should change his name as she had already had him for about six weeks, and he was used to Candy. She told the vet that she did not think he would mind having what was a rather girlie name. He wouldn't really know. The vet laughed, too, and chuckled. So Candy he remained. Candy is a name that Mum could remember from when she was a child and enjoyed a sweet called Coulter's Candy, which was striped red and white.

So Candy came home from the vet and settled in. He proceeded to destroy the wallpaper, to rip the lining of the curtains and to almost fly through the air as he jumped from place to place. After a while, because I now had a slim, trim figure and my muscles were coming back into operation, I started to fly around too. Ever since then, we normally have about two chases around the house each day. Because he is smaller, Candy can go higher. She can jump on top of the wardrobe on to a suitcase that lives up there. I am far too big to squeeze into the space between the suitcase and the ceiling, so he goes there when he wants to hide from visitors. Unlike Candy, I love visitors. Maybe he wants to just have peace and quiet. Or maybe to get away from me if I have been a bit too bossy.

Chapter 3

Terrible Teens Kitten

Candy has brought me lots of fun, and I love him very much. However, he had to learn a few rules, including some dos and don'ts. Once he had settled in and knew his way around, he started to become rather cheeky. Mum says that he would like to be an alpha male, whatever that is. He would definitely like to be a boss cat.

He has to learn that I was here first. I am older than he is, and I am a replacement for his mother on the farm. He cannot just boss me around. I am 'boss cat.' The first thing he has to learn is that there are rules, and I make the rules, not him.

I like to sleep on Mum's bed quite often. And most of the time, I am happy for him to sleep on it too. However, he cannot just assume that he can come onto the bed every night. Sometimes if we have had disagreements about something, and he jumps on the bed. I growl at him to go away. Mum does not get involved in these arguments. She leaves us to sort things out. Besides, most of the time she is not sure what we are quarrelling about anyway. Mum also reminds me that she does not mind Candy being on the bed, so I am to stop being nasty.

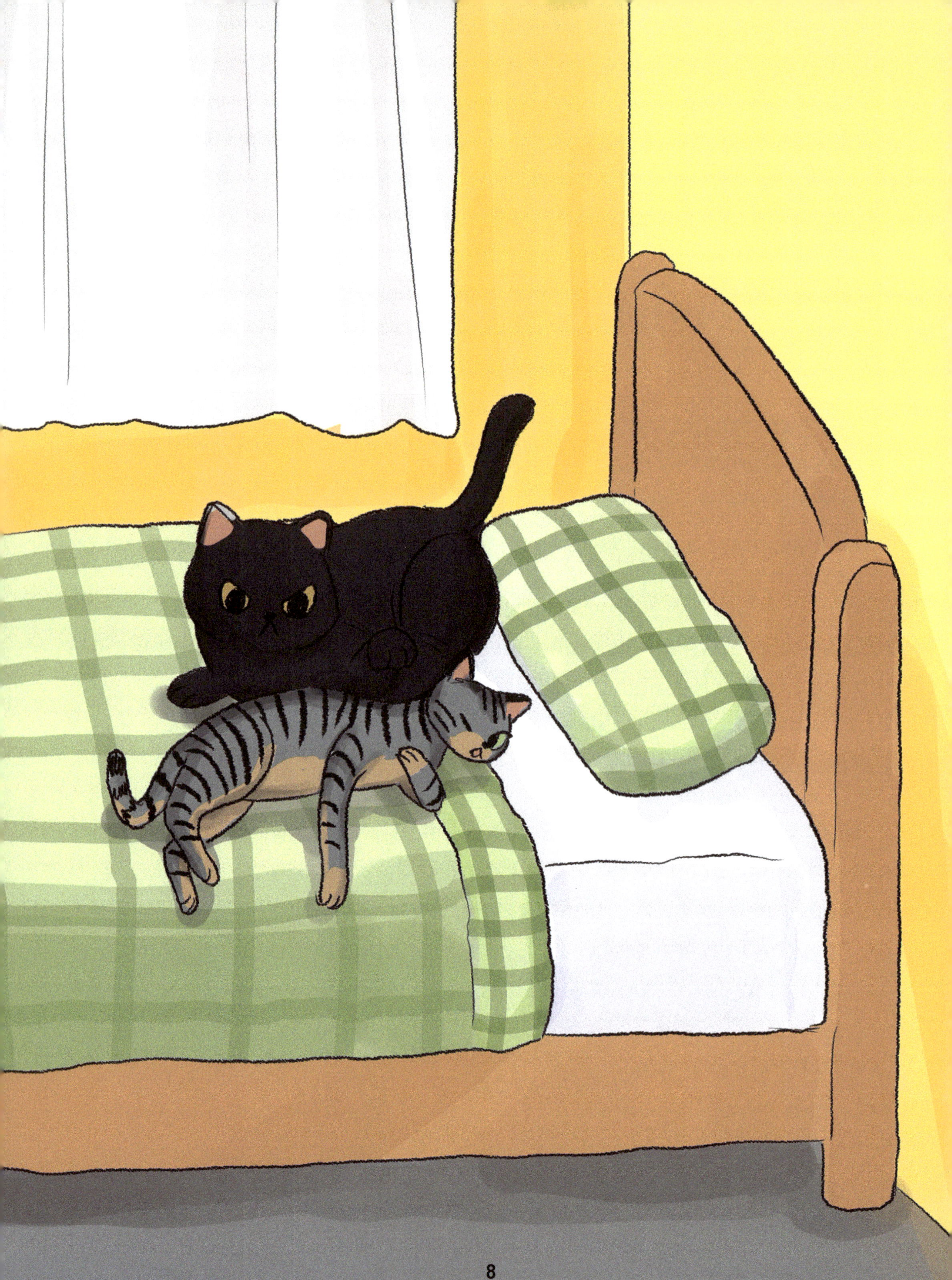

Something Candy does not want to understand is that I have rules as to who sleeps where on the bed. It is quite simple really. I cuddle into Mum, and he can cuddle into me. My favourite side is Mum's left, although I sometimes choose somewhere else. Sometimes he tries to push in between Mum and me. Now that is something I cannot allow. He is becoming rather cheeky and must be put in his place. I growl at him or sometimes hit him, hard. He has to learn!

It is particularly annoying if Candy tries that stunt after we have quarrelled during the evening! Candy must learn who is the boss around here, and it certainly is not him. I love him very much, but he really must learn his Ps and Qs. Most of the time he simply moves to the foot of the bed or to the other side. If I tell him to go away, he usually does. He knows I won't bear a grudge, so after a while, he comes back onto the bed very quietly and settles at the foot or on Mum's right side.

When we are getting on well, and he is not being a pest, I sometimes allow him to squeeze in between Mum and me. He really likes this, and he knows that I am allowing him to do so because he is behaving, and we are good friends.

Candy is a very talkative cat. He chats away, telling Mum that he wants to play with her or is hungry, which is all the time. If Mum goes into the kitchen, he assumes it is to feed him. I can think the same sometimes, but I don't make big noise about it. I do understand that Mum eats too.

Another thing that Candy does is to tell tales (not 'tails'). He likes to feel important, so he sometimes makes a big fuss if he thinks I am being naughty.

When he was still a teenage kitten, he started to kick up a real row one night, and he can be quite loud. Mum was having a nice, relaxing bath, but Candy made so much noise she really wondered whether there was something seriously wrong somewhere. She got out of the bath, and he shot ahead of her into the bedroom. I was on the bed, warming it up for Mum, and he was miaowing away and jumping around with a cheeky look on his face. Mum is quite sure he was saying, "Mollie is on the bed!"

Mum was telling a friend about it and used the word, 'cliping', a Scottish word that means 'telling tales'. She was telling this story in the doctor's waiting room, and the other patients there all started to titter. Yes, even grownups, as well as one little boy. The boy's dad really chortled!

Candy really does care about me. Sometimes—very occasionally—I wander out the front door and take a walk around our floor as far as the drying room. Sometimes I even go downstairs. I never go very far because the two doors on the ground floor, and even some of the doors to other wings, have what is called 'controlled entry'. So much as I would like to, I cannot get out into the garden. I am a very quiet cat, and Mum doesn't always miss me when she shuts the front door.

Then Candy will start to get very worried and upset, and he will chat away. After a while, Mum always realises he is really worried and will start to look for me. She works out what has happened and opens the door. I don't mind waiting on the doormat for a little while, but I am not totally silly. I sometimes scratch on the door. That sound, on top of Candy's excitable crying, gets action! I have never been out all that long, so I don't really mind.

I must explain that I am the one who has branded Candy a pest. Much as I love him, there are times when he really annoys me. One of those times is when I am trying to have a little sleep, what is actually called a *cat* nap.

Candy is a bundle of energy. He does not sleep as much as most cats, including me. Even when he is resting, he is really dozing but knows all that is going on. His ears keep moving, and he does not miss a trick. As soon as he is awake, usually before the crack of dawn, he thinks everyone else should be awake too. Mum says he is a bundle of nerves. He wakes up at the slightest sound or even movement! If Mum goes into the kitchen, he is running around, miaowing at her, and saying that he is hungry. He is always hungry, even the minute he has finished his meal. He does not understand that Mum has to eat too!

Today Candy managed to steal Mum's lunch. She turned away from the kitchen counter when the kettle boiled. And the instant her back was turned, he jumped soundlessly on to the counter and took two slices of cheese! Mum did not rise to be bait. She simply divided what was left in two and put them into our dishes. I did not manage to eat all my helping, so he finished it off for me! What a pest!

Another thing he does not understand is that a lady like me needs her beauty sleep. Sometimes I wake up first in the morning so that I am first on the bed, even if I have spent the night in the living room. However, I do need to have a good sleep until it is close to time for Mum to get up. When I have this sleep, I really sleep. I curl up, nose to tail, and have a nice, deep sleep. Candy does not approve of this and tries to wake me up. When he succeeds, it makes me very cross!

We also have disagreements Mum cannot quite understand. Sometimes we suddenly flash our tails and glare at each other. We even spit or hit each other sometimes. Actually, I am the one who does most of the hitting. I have big paws and quite regularly box his ears, which is what a mother cat—or a boss cat—does. They know that kittens and even younger adults need to be reminded now and again who is the boss. These little spats are soon over, and neither of us carries grudges.

There is one area in which Candy is the boss. Mum says he is more streetwise than I am. Mum says that maybe that should be 'farm wise.' Whatever it is, Candy has persuaded me to do naughty things that would have *never* entered my head before he came along. Some of these things are great fun, and I love to join in.

Chapter 4

Planning and Plotting

Life as a sole cat in a small flat is very quiet. I had some toys to play with, but I did not really bother about them unless Mum decided to play with them. And I certainly did not try to steal food. This is something I now try to do on a regular basis.

People who do not know much about cats think that we are dumb animals in the sense that we don't talk to each other. Anyone who knows anything at all is well aware that we can talk to each other without making a sound. Sometimes when I am on the bed and Candy comes in, we have a discussion without making any sounds, and I follow him into the living room or the kitchen. Candy has noticed something that I would have missed, and he likes to be a stirrer.

Before Candy came along, Mum left the kitchen door open at night so that I could go in and have a drink of water if I wanted to. The same thing happened when she went out to the shops or wherever she was going, and I would just settle down to have a catnap.

Candy had other ideas. He wanted to create some excitement, so he told me what we could do. One of our favourite games was to open the larder door and knock boxes of cat food off the shelf. Then we had great fun ripping open the big

14

box with our claws and then tearing the little pouches of meat to pieces, eating the meat and leaving the bits and pieces on the floor while we went for a joint cat nap. Mum would come home and get rather annoyed when she saw what we had done. She would get wound up and talk about the fact that "Money doesn't grow on trees," and that we left the mess, "For the maid to clean up!" Yes, that was the fun part, watching her getting wound up! Then Mum decided to take drastic measures. She picked up two tins from a pet shop one Christmas to hold the boxes of cat food. We cannot break into them even if we do manage to open the larder door.

Candy came up with another really good, idea which is just as much fun. Mum is very keen on something called recycling. She puts all sorts of bits and pieces into a bag which hangs on the larder door. Every so often she takes a bagful to the recycling bin in the garden. Among the bits and pieces are the empty pouches that the cat food was in. But they are not really completely empty; there are always little bits of meat stuck in corners or onto the foil packaging. Once Candy suggested it and showed me what to do a few times, I became expert at opening these packets. I'm a big, strong girl with very strong claws, so I am much better than Candy at ripping the packages apart. After the fun of opening the packet, I eat the meat that is left inside. Wouldn't it be silly to let it go to waste? And once again, it is great fun to watch Mum pick up the mess. When she is *really* wound up we hear her saying, "That bad cat!" We are not sure who the bad cat is, but we have a good idea that it is Candy or me, maybe both! It is good fun, and it would be a shame to waste all those pieces of cat food now, wouldn't it?

One good thing I do, and that Candy has never tried, is to bring in the mail from the front door. When I started doing this, Mum was puzzled. She couldn't remember taking an envelope into the kitchen, but there it was, lying in the middle of the floor, in perfect condition. I *never* tear up the mail. After a while, she realised I was being helpful.

In cat terms, I was also showing respect towards my boss cat. A group of feral cats, or truly wild cats, always has a boss cat, and the other members of the group show their respect to him or her by bringing presents. In a flat there are no places where I can hunt for a present, so I bring in a letter from the hall to the kitchen, where Mum will find it as soon as she comes back from wherever she has been. I am showing *my* respect for the boss cat, Mum. Candy has never done that, ever.

Mum sometimes forgets to shut the kitchen door at night, usually when she is very tired. Normally I don't notice straightaway because I am so busy settling down for a sleep. Cat or not, I know that most of the night, at least until dawn, is used by humans to sleep, so I might as well do the same.

This is when Candy will come onto the bed, or simply to the bedroom door, and start to miaow loudly to tell me that we can have some fun! Then he will come into the room, not always onto the bed, and we have one of our silent conversations. Mum will see me disappear out the bedroom, but because she is tired, she doesn't bother about it. Then we have great fun in the kitchen, demolishing the recycling bag and checking what is in it.

After we have had that game, I quite often have a guilty conscience and do not go back into the bedroom until Candy announces that it is time to get up. Sometimes not even then. When Candy has done something wrong, it doesn't seem to bother him that he might get into trouble. Perhaps he was dragged and not brought up on the farm. The only thing he has stopped doing because he knows it is naughty—and because there is no wallpaper left within his reach—is to sharpen his claws on the wallpaper. Mum is not sure she will replace it because he might decide that it would be great fun to get rid of it too. We do have a cat post, but we do not use it very often. Wallpaper is *much* better. Well, until there is none left, at least not where we can reach! To be fair, even before Candy arrived, I had a few goes at the wallpaper, but I never reached as far up the wall as he does. Candy likes to reach up high, so he jumps onto furniture. He probably thinks, *Why not? Isn't that what furniture is for, to practise the high jump?*

I have decided to copy Candy with something that I had never done until this winter. I sleep on the night storage heater in the hall. Candy, poor boy, feels the cold. One of his favourite spots is the storage heater in the living room. A couple of weeks ago I decided to test out the one in the hall. It is nice and comfy, and it is quite long enough for me to stretch out and toast my tummy. It is *very* nice. It also means I can keep nice and warm whilst I am waiting for Mum to come home as I do like to go into the hall to meet her.

Chapter 5

Computer Capers

There is a machine in our house that I don't quite approve of. I am not sure what it does, but I do know that I become jealous of it when Mum spends time using it instead of cuddling me!

Actually, Mum becomes annoyed with it sometimes because it does not always do what she wants it to. That makes her hopping mad! Candy and I both know to keep out of the way when Mum is upset with the computer. She becomes *really* upset and sometimes ends up crying. Sometimes she dislikes the computer as much as I do, but that is because it won't do as it is told!

When we wake up from our afternoon catnaps and decide that it is time to have our supper, we are much happier if Mum is watching the news or something on television than if she is busy on that machine. Sometimes she becomes so absorbed in what she is doing on the computer that she cannot stop, not even when Candy starts to complain. And believe me, when Candy starts to complain, it gets louder and louder until it is positively ear-splitting! I mean *ear*-splitting because he has a very shrill voice, and it really grates on one's ears! Mum often says it is amazing that such a tiny little cat can make so much noise! I am usually very quiet. Even when it is suppertime, I purr most of the time or miaow nicely, just a tiny little "Miaow." Mum really likes that. One noisy cat is enough.

I heard Mum say once that Siamese cats make a loud noise. That makes sense because long ago, Siamese cats were guard cats in the royal palaces in a place called Thailand. It must have been inside the palace because Siamese cats really like to be comfortable. And like Candy, they want to boss other cats.

A few nights ago Mum was having computer problems when she was trying to do something called online banking. She was really quite stressed out. Candy was becoming stressed too because he was impatiently waiting for his supper. Mum was nearly crying from frustration because the computer would not do as it was told. While she was struggling with this problem, Candy's miaowing became louder and louder. One would think he had never been fed! Really, he did go on! Eventually not only Mum was fed up, but I was too. Mum had told him to be quiet several times. And he should have known she was upset, though he doesn't notice such things. I finally decided that enough was enough. I *growled* at him, loudly, and boxed his ears. He was stunned into silence! You see, he ignores Mum, but he knows I am boss cat. Mum was most impressed! The silence was deafening!

When I think Mum has spent too much time pounding away on the computer, I jump on the desk and walk straight across the keyboard in front of her. Sometimes my paws hit the letters, and Mum has to get rid of them, by which time I have turned round and started walking back across the keyboard in the opposite direction. I am usually purring, so Mum knows I am just asking her to stop and give me a cuddle or play a game, so she does not get bothered by it. She will take a break, and I jump down from the desk, and rub myself against her legs, the way cats do, and Mum likes it.

Candy is not bothered by Mum working on the computer. In fact, he takes no interest in the keyboard part at all. What he does like is the thing called a printer. He likes it because it is up high, so he can sit up there and look around. He never tries to do the high jump whilst Mum is sitting in her chair. He likes to do it when he can take a running jump onto the desk, and almost immediately, almost without stopping for breath, he springs up in the air and flies in front of the screen, gradually rising higher and higher, and lands on the flat top of the printer. He looks beautiful when he does it, so graceful and pretty, just like an acrobat.

Once he is up on top of the printer he sits there, looking around and thoroughly enjoying himself.

When he has been up there long enough for his liking, he springs off the printer. Sometimes he lands on the desk for a second. But on other occasions, he jumps straight from the printer to the floor. He likes to do it the second way when Mum is relaxing, watching the television, or listening to music. Sometimes when he springs from the top of the printer, it makes quite a big noise. I suppose printers have not really been designed to be springboards, so it complains, and maybe his claws scratch the metal. If Mum is absorbed in what she is doing, the noise makes her jump. Candy thinks that is fun!

Chapter 6

Lockdown

I started writing this book during something called "lockdown". I have heard that word a lot recently on the News on the radio and television. Mum is always *very* interested in the news.

I do not really know what a lockdown is, but it does mean that Mum is here at home much more than she used to be. That is good, although it is more difficult to get up to mischief.

Candy was six—yes, six—in November. He is starting to grow up quite a bit. He no longer climbs up the curtains, that luckily are lined. We have had to get used to the fact that sometimes Mum is only away for an hour or two. Whatever lockdown is, it has changed Mum's life quite a lot. We know that sometimes she becomes fed up with lockdown. She says that everyone is fed up with it, but it is just something we have to do until the virus (whatever a virus is) goes away. I have heard Mum say that she would, "Go off my trolley", if she didn't have her cats. She is not someone who likes to be on her own all that much, although she has lived alone for a long time.

Whatever lockdown is, it became exciting on New Year's Day. At nine in the morning there was a knock at the door. Mum thought it might be someone 'first footing' her, whatever that is. It turned out to be the lady in the flat below us. She had water pouring through the ceiling down into the shower. She had already spoken to the emergency department at somewhere called 'City Building'. Well, that was when the action started! Mum's first action was to phone 'City Building', who said that a plumber was on his way.

A plumber arrived very quickly, soon after Mum put down the phone actually. He didn't stay long, but then another man arrived, and he stayed. In fact, I wondered whether he was going to stay here forever. He was a busy man, running up and down between two flats. It was dark by the time he found the leak. Mum jokingly said to him at about eight o'clock in the evening, "The way things are going, you will soon be starting the night shift."

He was a very nice man and said, "If I have to I will. I am determined to find it. That poor woman downstairs still has water pouring down."

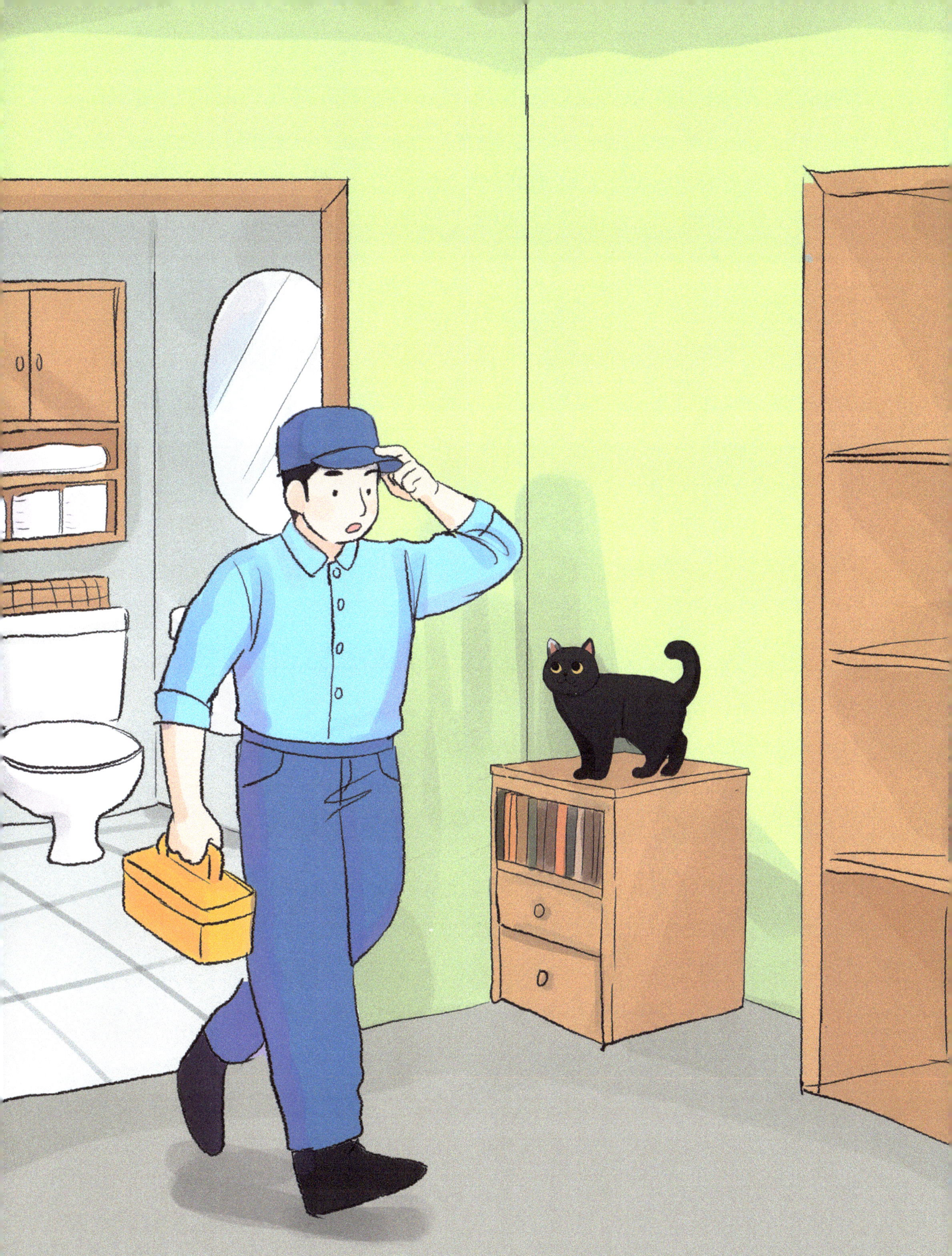

Then the night shift did turn up, two more large men, so there were three men in my flat at one time! I had never seen that before! Mum even joked about it the next day with a neighbour, saying, with a bit of a chuckle, that she had three tall young men in her flat on New Year's Day! He laughed too.

Anyway, the plumber started work again. He took away the skirting board on one side of the bathroom and started to fiddle around. Then he went into the big cupboard and went over to the hot water tank. He listened to the water in the pipes. He was very happy. He had found the source of the leak in a pipe that ran under the floor to the bath. Then he discovered that there might be asbestos in the tiles on the floor, so he couldn't do anymore until the asbestos team, whoever they are, had been. Then he switched off the water— yes, all of it—and phoned City Building to tell them to send bottled water.

That plumber was a very nice man. He worked all weekend, coming back on Sunday because the lady downstairs still had water coming down. Then he fiddled with some more things in the big cupboard including parts of the pipes running from the back wall that were close to and part of the hot water tank.

Oh, yes, Mum says that one of the cats she had before me, a cat whose mistress had been taken seriously ill, found the hot tank very quickly and used to toast himself on it. Candy feels the cold, too, but he has had to make do with the radiator because he hasn't found the hot water tank yet. It is unusual for him to miss anything.

The bottles of water arrived on Sunday, lots of them. We needed them too. We had no running

24

water all last week because the technician did not come until Friday! Then he took away something from our floor and sent it away to a lab. Whatever happened at the lab took a long time, and we still had no running water. Mum used a lot of bottled water one way and the other. She missed nice warm baths.

I am curious about the bath and the shower. I sometimes watch Mum when she is in the bath and become quite worried in case something serious happens to her. I even put my paws up on the edge of the tub and take a good look at the water and the bubbly stuff that is in it.

I use the bath when it is empty. We have a sunny bathroom, and the bath is made of some kind of plastic that becomes nice and warm on sunny days. I have also found that the wash basin is a nice snug place for me to curl up in. It is just the right size to make me feel safe and comfy. Mum says she will take a photo of me in it one of these days.

During lockdown, since Christmas, we have had some very dark mornings. Sometimes Candy and I think it is still the middle of the night and wake up much later than usual. On other occasions, I wake up at about four in the morning and move into Mum's bed. I fall into another deep sleep, feeling nice and cosy. Then the pest comes in when he wakes up and starts to miaow away, saying it is time to be up! He thinks that just because he is up everyone else should get up as well. Sometimes he even comes onto the bed and pokes his paw into me, which makes me *really* angry. I growl at him to go away, and if he doesn't, I spit, hiss, and sometimes even hit him hard. I mean to say, what is the point of getting up on a dark, cold morning?

Chapter 7

Aunties

I have aunties who come to visit us when Mum is away for something called 'holidays' or another place called 'hospital', that is not so much fun and has not been planned.

Although I am not as cluey as Candy, I do know that a suitcase means something is going to happen. Mum puts clothes into the case and then closes it. It makes a nice bed for me to lie on, and I can also keep a close eye on what Mum is doing. If it is a big case, it means she is going on holiday. If it is a tiny one, which I don't usually get time to lie on, it means hospital.

I don't like Mum to disappear without me noticing, but it does seem to happen. I often find that she has gone whilst I have been asleep in the living room or even on the bed. When I wake up, Candy and I are on our own until one of our aunties arrives.

Our aunties come in to see that we are well and happy. They feed us, take photos to send to Mum by mobile phone, and play with us. Sometimes, if we are fretting for Mum, they bring us little treats. These aunties are very nice ladies. One Christmas an auntie sent her husband instead, and he fixed the vacuum cleaner (which I hated). That one wasn't around for much longer, and Mum bought one that does not make so much racket.

27

The aunties have also come when Mum is in hospital. They send Mum messages on the mobile phone to tell her that we are fine. The aunties have been coming in to visit Mum's cats for eleven years. It is much nicer to stay at home than to go to a cattery. I know that other cats go away on holiday with their owners. Mum's childhood cat was one of them. Mum also met a cat who was in his carrier on the ferry to Belfast. Those cats are usually visiting relatives. Our mum usually goes away for ten days or two weeks. However, a couple of years ago she went away for a month to a place called Australia. We were happy to have our aunties coming in.

Chapter 8

Visits to the Vet

Candy and I are both very healthy. However, Mum has to watch my weight. I am a greedy girl and liable to put on the pounds. I am sure I will have gained weight during this lockdown, just like everyone else. The main problem is that I did not manage to make it to my annual check-up.

Mum and I travel to the vet by taxi. I am in my carrier. Unlike a lot of cats, I am quite happy to go into mine. It is nice and cosy, and I can see what is going on. It doesn't take long for the taxi to reach the PDSA (People's Dispensary for Sick Animals).

It is *very* busy in there! Mainly dogs and cats, but there are sometimes rabbits and other small pets; hamsters are very popular too. Sometimes the waiting room is very noisy with people talking, dogs barking, and general clatter. Occasionally a couple of dogs take a dislike to each other, and they kick up a terrific row. Usually the owner of the loudest, angriest dog takes him (it is usually a him) outside until their name is called, or there is more room and the two dogs don't need to sit next to each other. Normally I don't mind because I am nice and safe in my carrier, and Mum is right next to me.

When I hear the name "Mollie" called, I know that I am going into a small room called a surgery. I normally enjoy seeing the vet, usually a lady, and I come out of my carrier and preen myself, showing her what a big beautiful girl I am. Then she puts me onto the scales and tells Mum that she has been good about watching my weight. Then she looks at my eyes, and ears, and prods various parts of my body very gently. I have always been very healthy, so I do not need any medicine at the moment. The last thing the vet does is put a tiny needle through my fur and into my neck; I hardly feel a thing. Usually when the vet tells me I am a good girl I purr loudly and go into my carrier without any fuss.

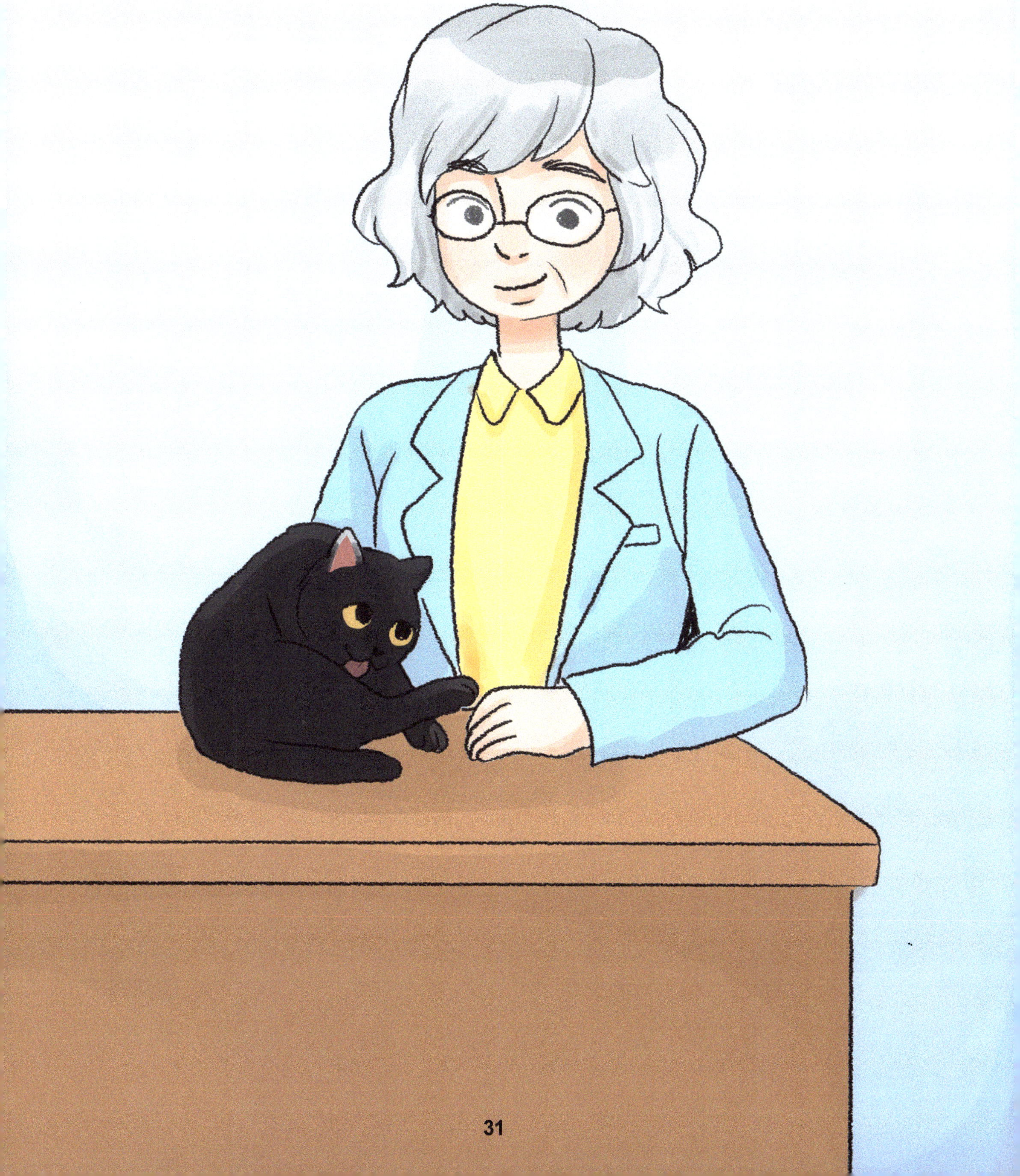

The last time was different. The waiting room was noisier than ever. I think the vets were busy with animals that were really ill, not just in for a check-up like me. I got really fed up. We waited for ages before I heard, "Mollie". When I went into the surgery, I was very grumpy. I growled when the vet put her hand into the carrier to stroke me, and for the first time ever, I refused to come out. The vet was very nice about it. She told Mum that I was upset because of the noise, and I would be tired. Mum said, "Tired, what has made her tired? She hasn't been doing anything very energetic!" The vet explained that the long wait and the noise would have been just too much for me. We did get the weigh-in completed and my shot. And once again the vet was pleased that I was such a slim, trim girl.

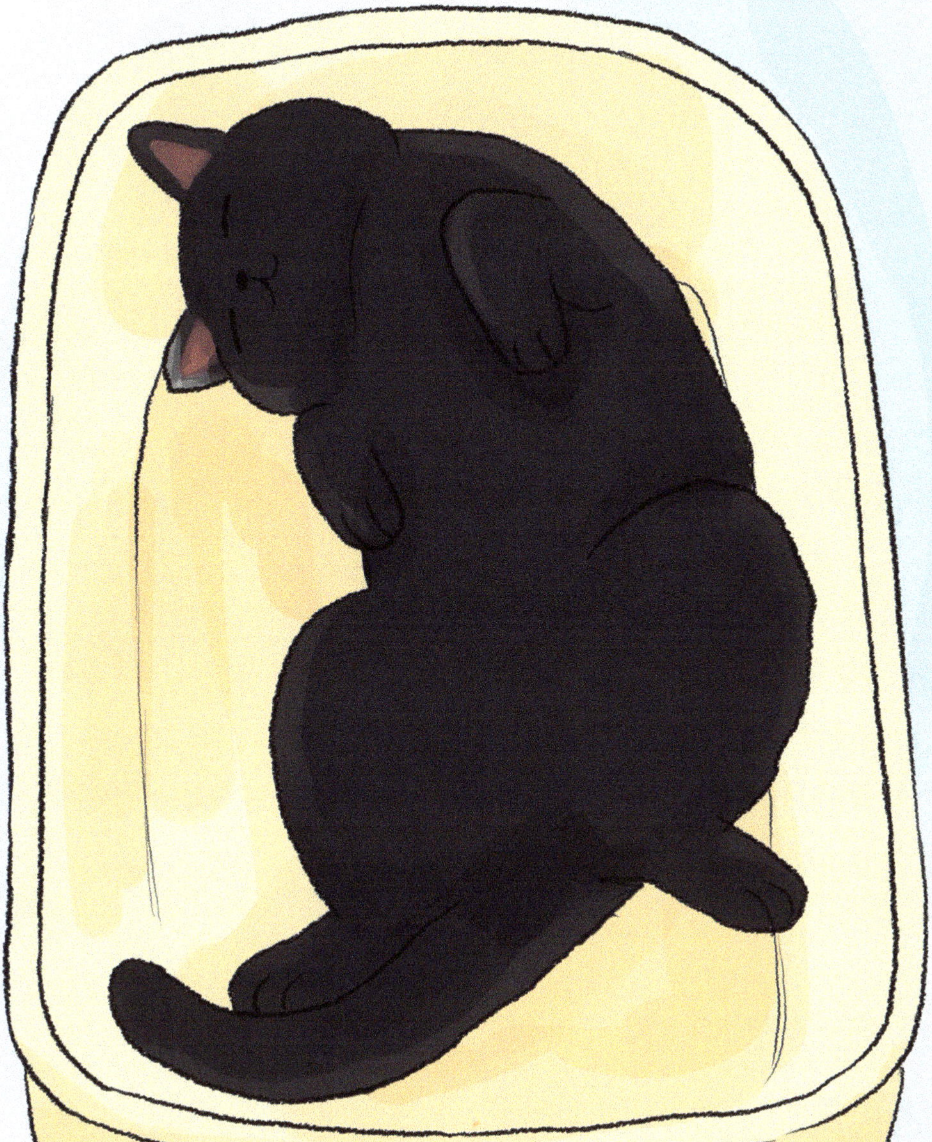

Then she asked Mum about Candy, who has never been back since he had a shot as a kitten. Mum explained that she just couldn't catch him, much less put him in the carrier. "He would be hanging on the chandeliers if I tried to put him into the carrier. I am just not up to catching him!"

We all agreed that he must be healthy. Mum assured the vet that she was sure she would notice if Candy was ill because he wouldn't be flying around the way he does. It was very embarrassing, really, to have to explain to the vet why he wouldn't come.

Chapter 9

Cheerio for Now

Now I have told you about the things I do and some of my thoughts about the life of two pussies. We have great times together, and it has done us both good to have each other for company.

Candy must think he is living in great comfort, having come from a farmyard, even though some farmyards can be quite comfy. Cats are great survivors and can be found in the most unexpected places. There was one on the television a few nights ago who has made his home on a nature reserve, where he lives in the office building. For many years a cat lived in the People's Palace in Glasgow, and when she died (aged twenty-three, I think), the staff laid a memorial stone in her memory. You can see it in the ground just outside the Winter Garden.

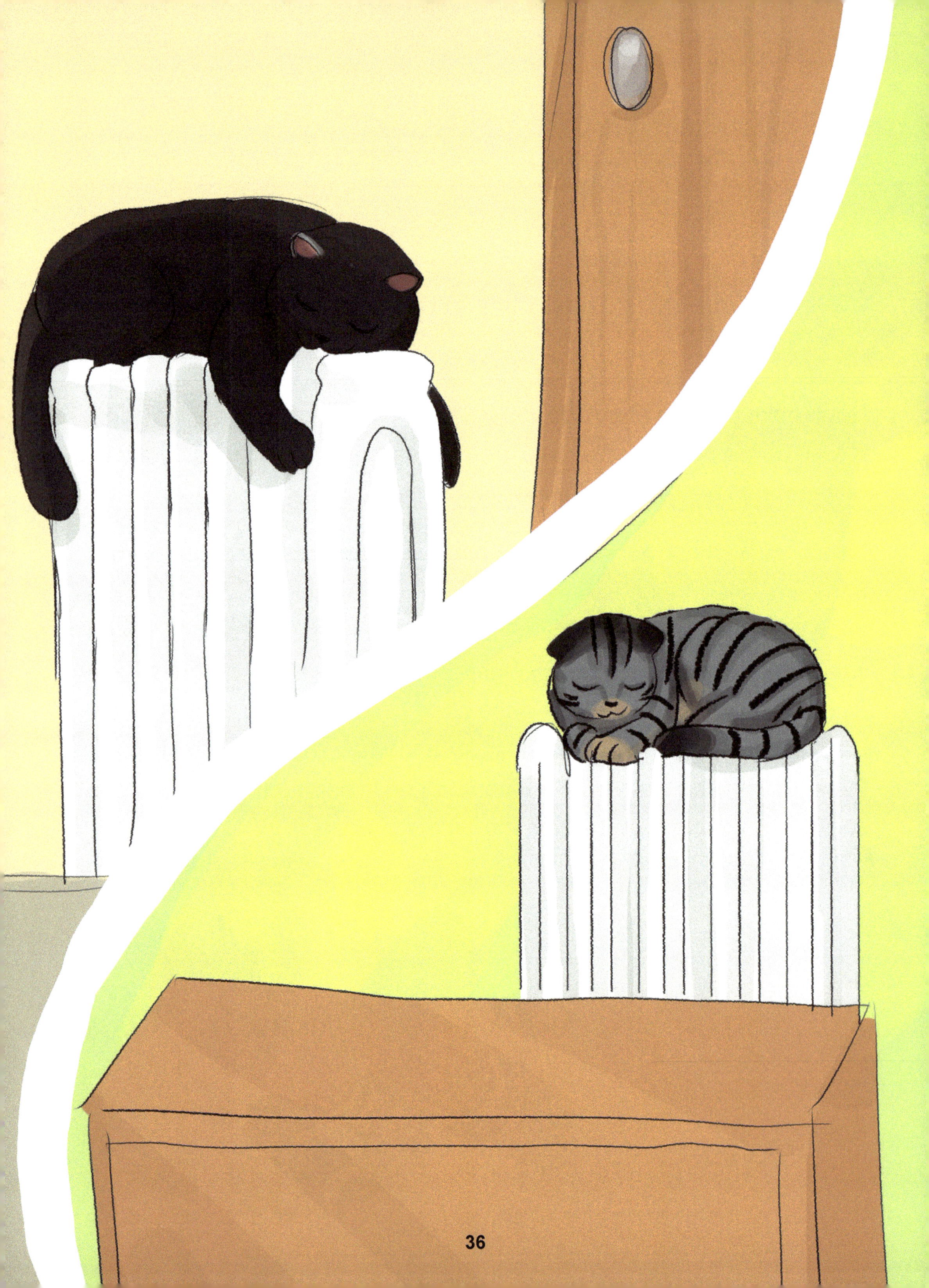

I am lucky in one respect. When the people who had me as a kitten decided three years later that I, "didn't do anything", they took me to Cats Protection. So of course Cats Protection is one of my favourite charities. Mum supports them regularly. I think I will send them an up-to-date photo of myself so that they can see that I am a slim, trim, beautiful girl. Candy and I cannot go into the garden, but we do have a nice life here.

I hope you have enjoyed my miaowsings and that they will make you feel happy. You never know, I might come back with more later. So cheerio for now.

Mollie and Candy (the pest) say goodbye for now. I do mean it kindly when I call him 'the pest'; we are good friends, even if we do fall out from time to time.

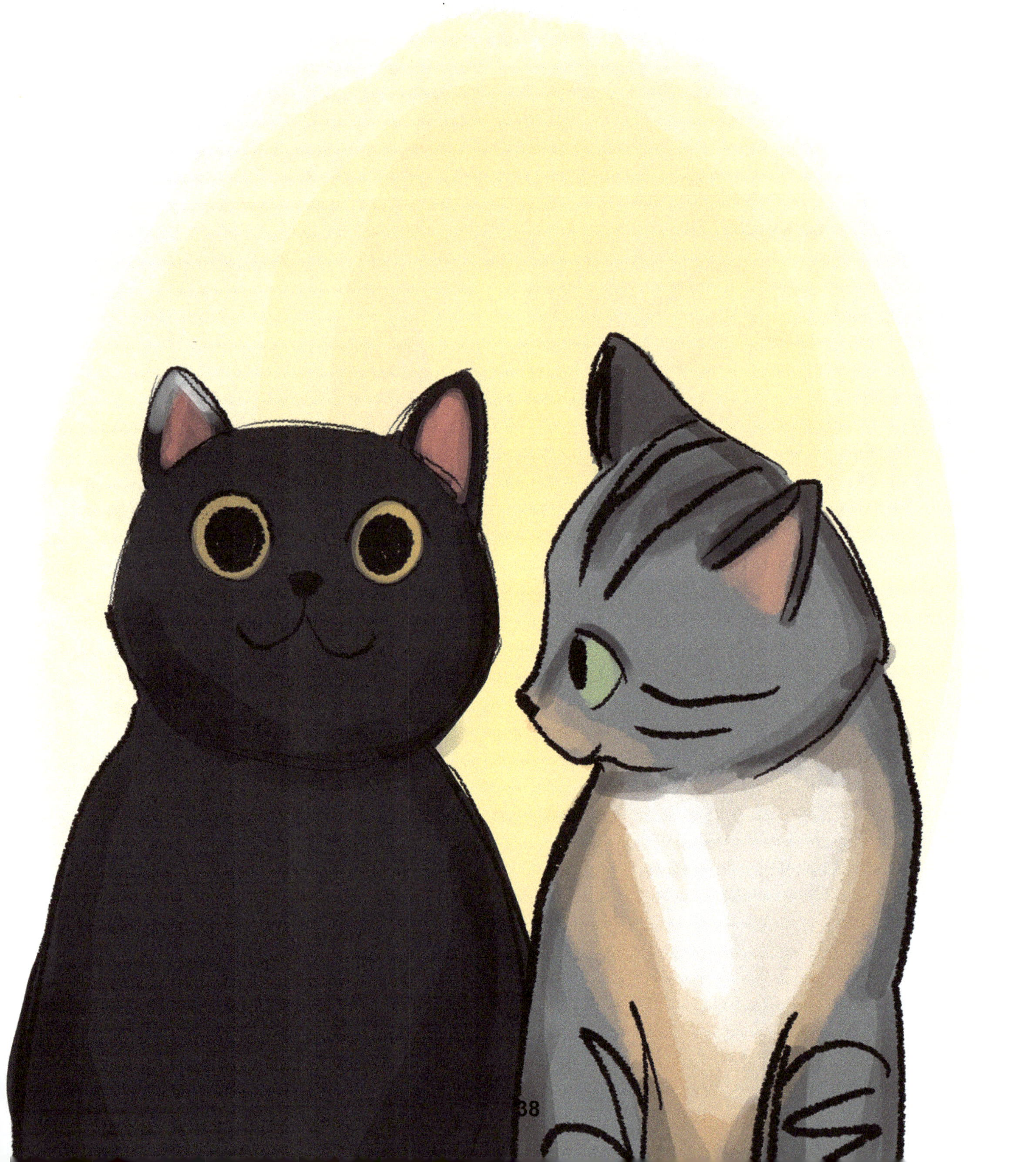

Photos of Mollie and Candy

Mollie and Candy

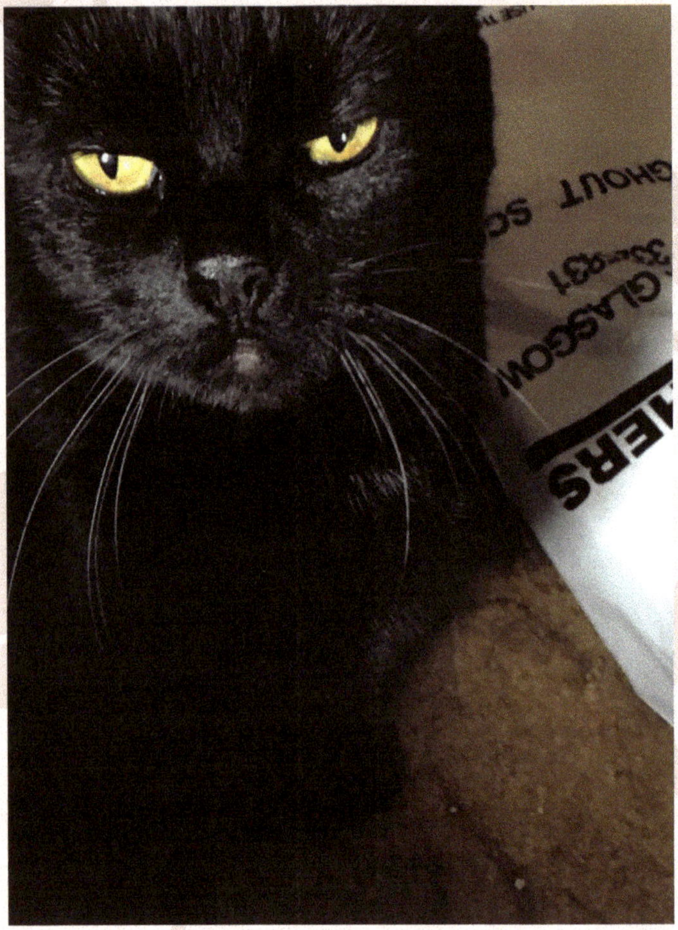

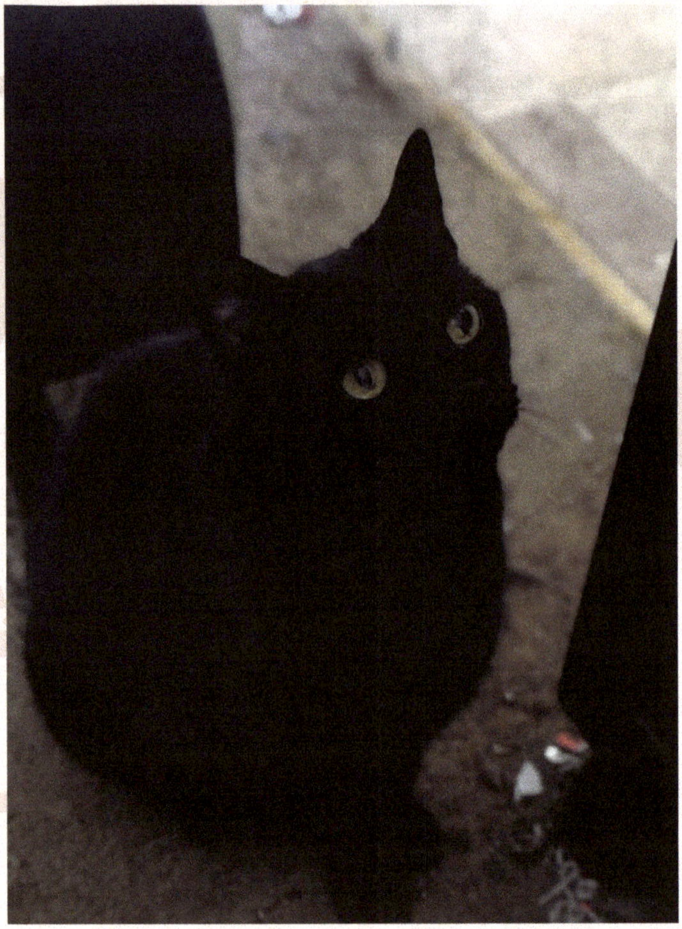

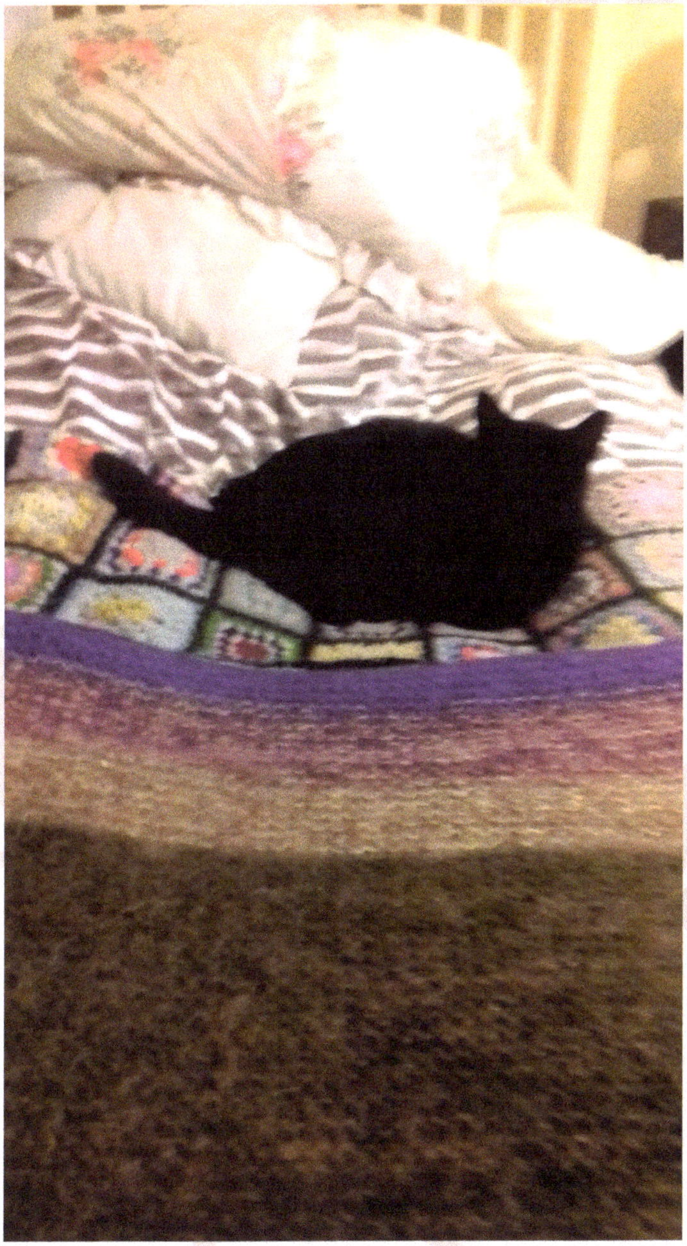

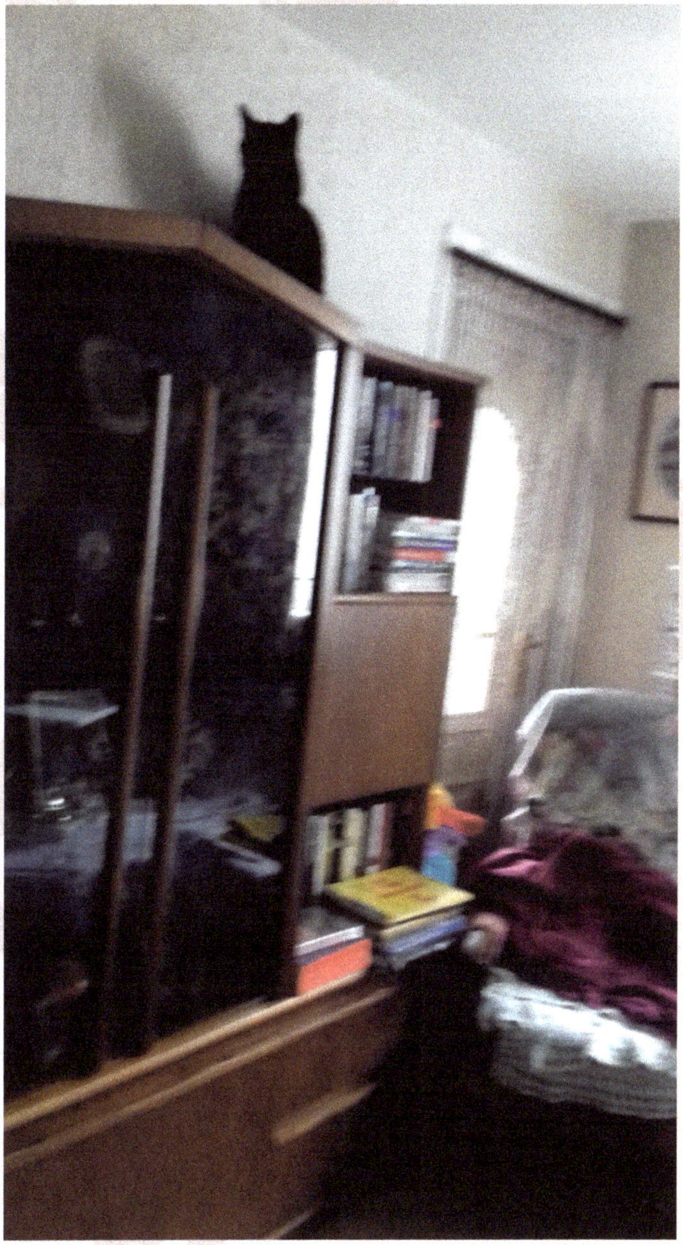

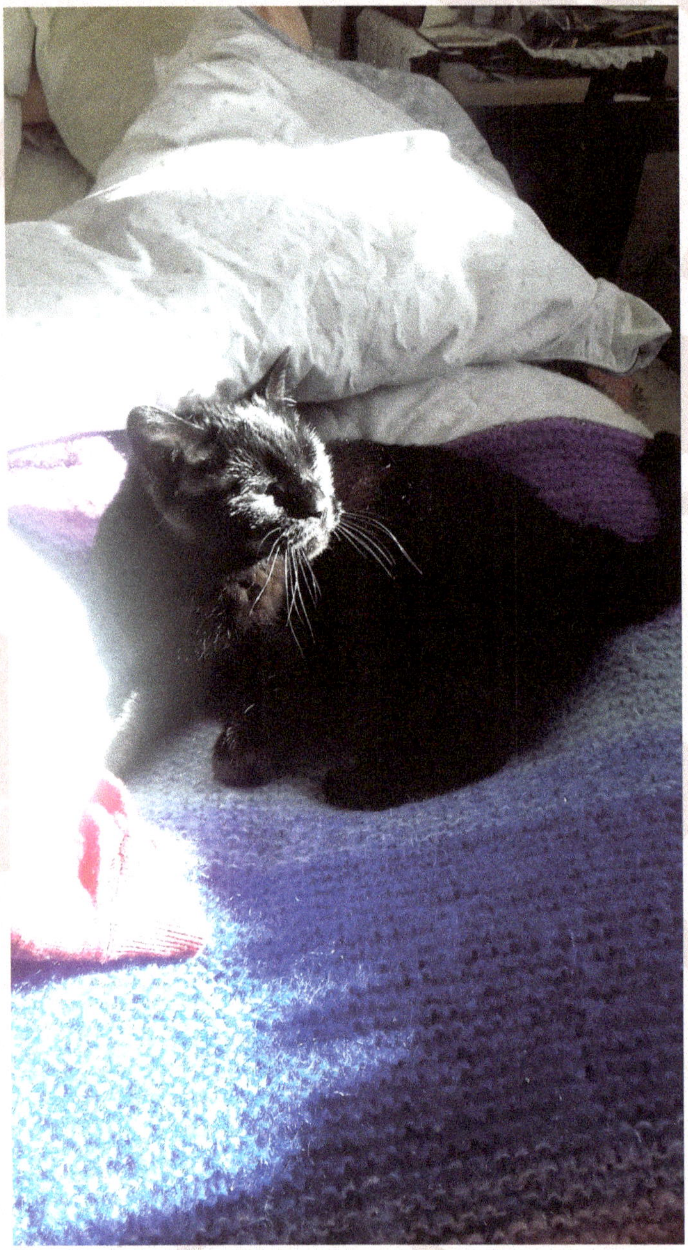

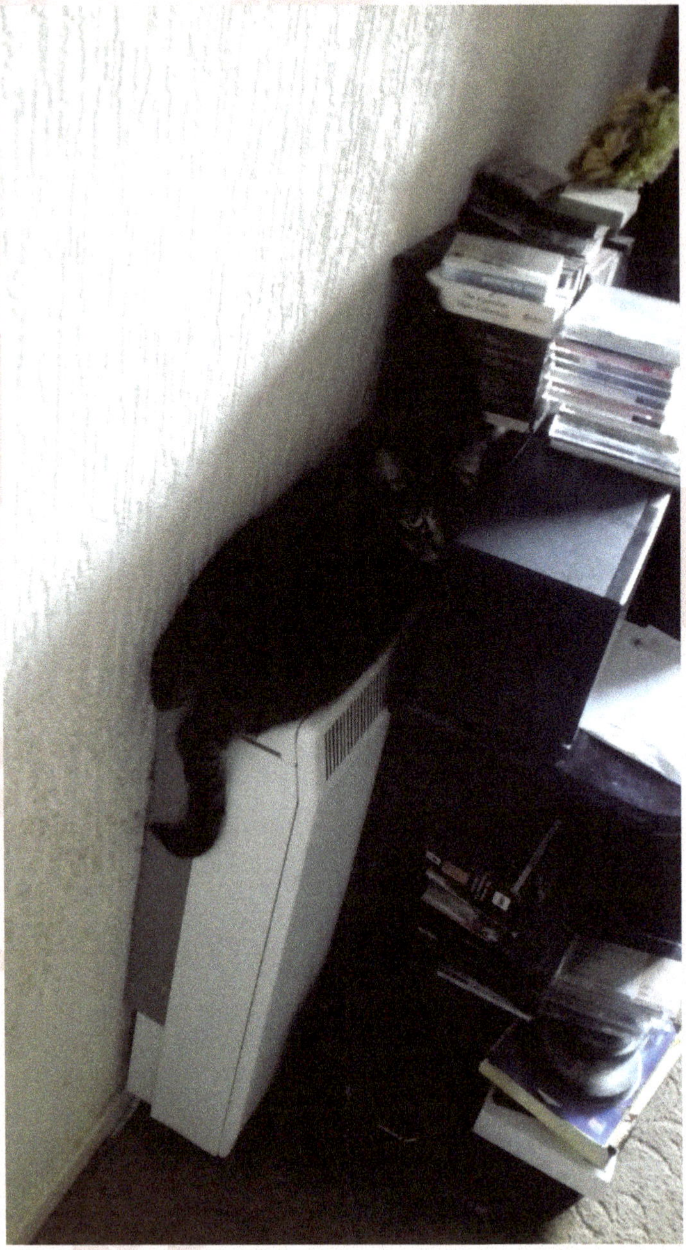

43

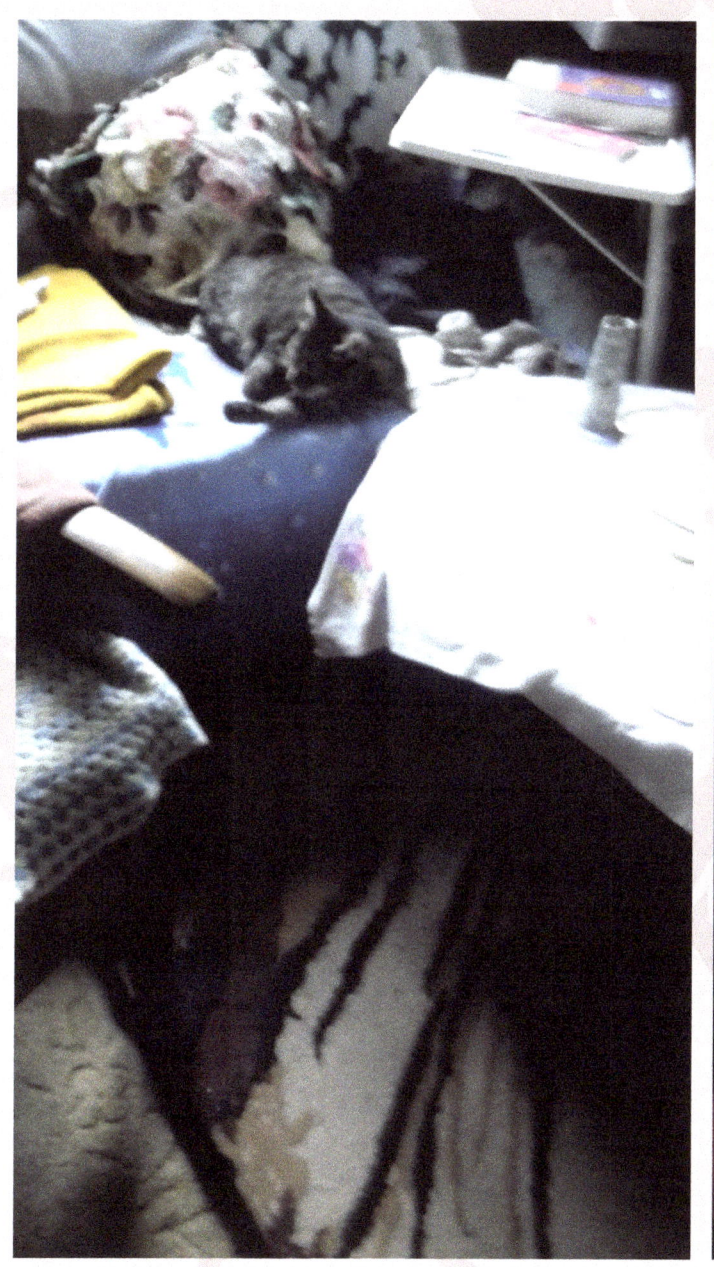

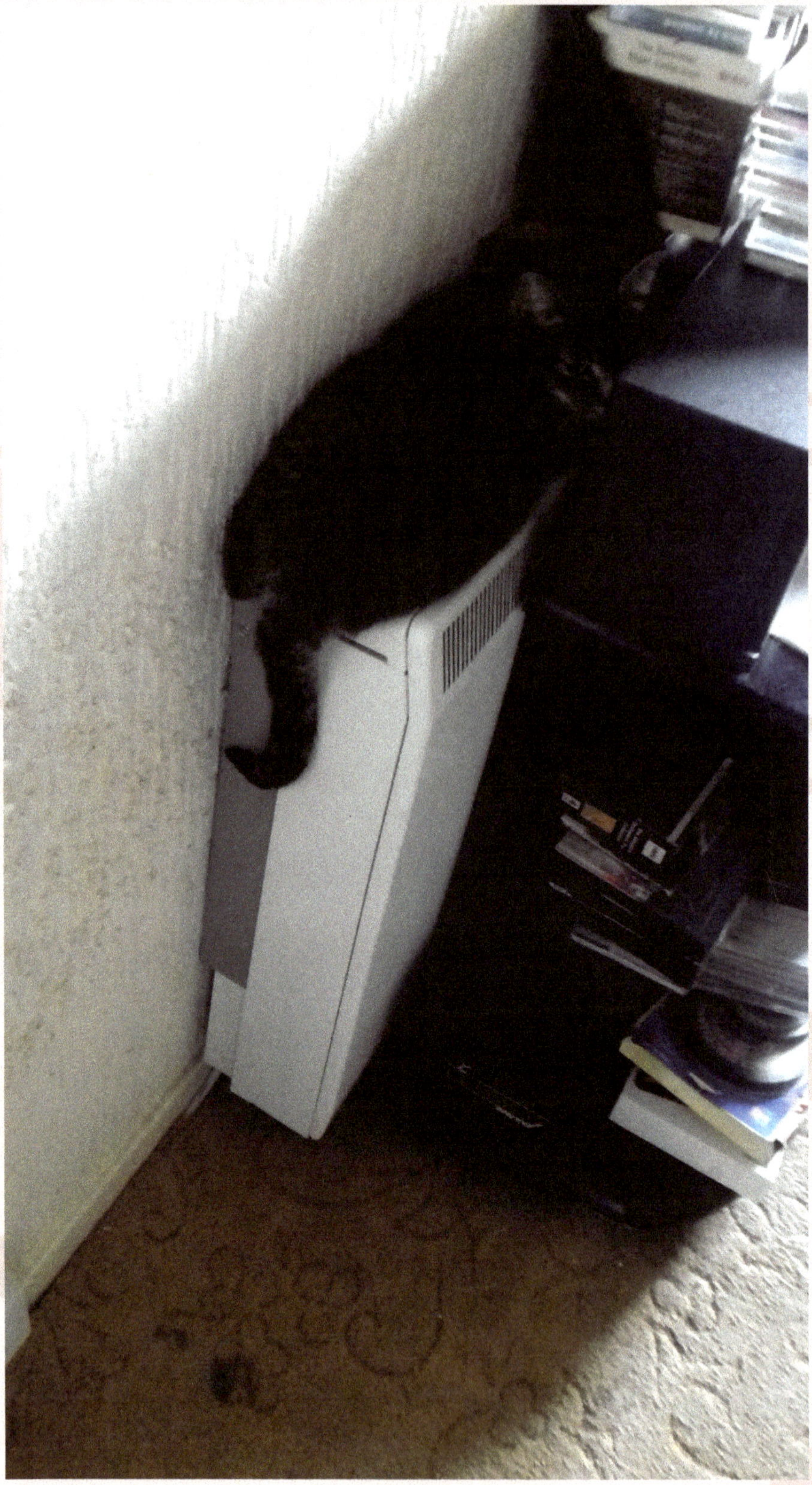

45

CPSIA information can be obtained
at www.ICGtesting.com
Printed in the USA
LVHW011534130623
749656LV00013B/280

9 781982 284947